DEVOTIONAL

PREPARE
HIM ROOM

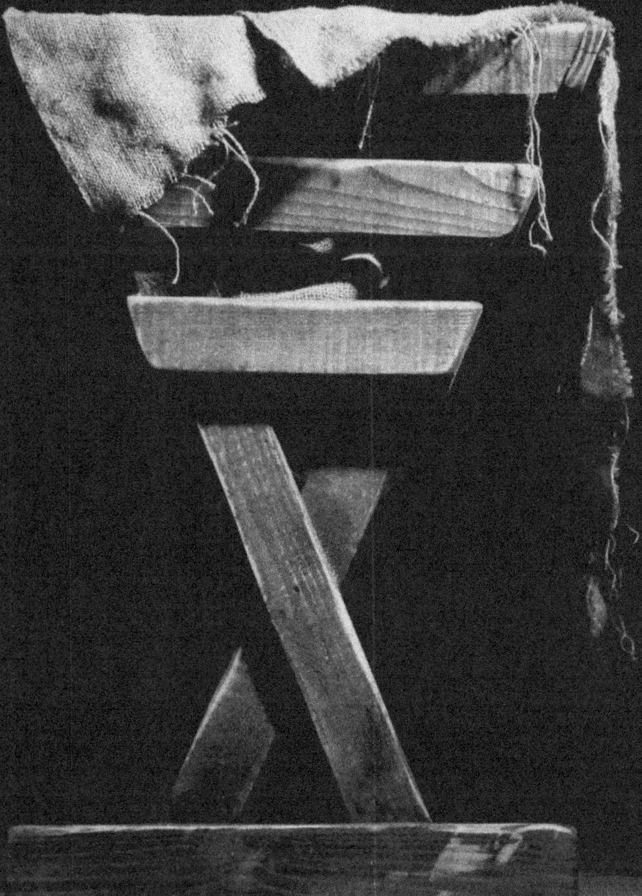

ALSO BY RUTH HOVSEPIAN

100 Days of Prayer: a journey into *deeper intimacy* with GOD

100 Days of Prayer: Prayer Journal Edition

The Ultimate Conversation: Is that you, GOD?

A Mother's Love: A Heartfelt Journey

Edited by Andrea Lende
Cover and Interior Design by Ruth Hovsepian

ISBN: 978-1-962581-45-5 (print)
ISBN: 978-1-962581-46-2 (ebook)

ACKNOWLEDGEMENTS

Thank you, GOD, for your awesome gift of GRACE.

DEDICATION

Andrea Lende, thank you, my dear, sweet sister-friend, who encourages me and sees something in me that I cannot. Thank you for your prayers, for being a sounding board, and for laughing at my crazy ideas! Your stewardship and faithfulness will not go unrewarded.

Whatever is good and perfect is a gift coming down to us from God our Father, who created all the lights in the heavens.

James 1:17 (NLT)

DEVOTIONAL

PREPARE HIM ROOM

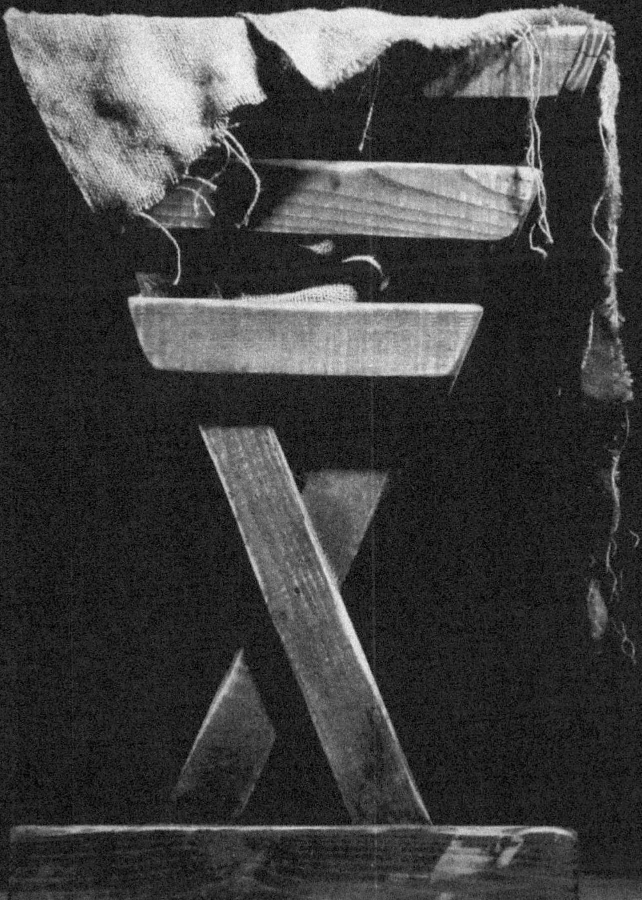

Contents

A NOTE FROM RUTH

M ay this book help you enjoy God's priceless gift to us—His only Son, Jesus, born in a stable and laid in a manger. As we celebrate the birth of Jesus Christ, let us remember that He came into the world to give eternal life to all who believe in Him.

I will be praying for readers of Prepare Him Room. Remember that Jesus is Immanuel, God with us. May you enjoy His peace and His presence in ever-increasing measure.

A peaceful and joyous Christmas!

Ruth Horsepian

BEFORE YOU BEGIN

C hristmas is one of my favorite times of year because I am in-spired to intentionally reflect on the divine birth of our Lord and Savior. However, if you're like me, the Holiness of Christ's birth can get lost in the hustle and bustle of the Christmas season. While it should be the most revered and joy-filled time of year, I struggle to maintain this viewpoint, and it passes before I realize what has happened. I want to recognize and celebrate this sacred season and pray you will experience it, too.

These daily devotions gently guide you through reflection and cel-ebration this holiday season, inviting you to slow down, pause, and focus on the true meaning of Christmas.

Within these pages, I offer a holistic approach to celebrating Christ-mas. You will be encouraged to align your heart and actions with the message of Jesus' birth, allowing His love, grace, and forgiveness to shape your interactions with others. You will be challenged to embrace the values of compassion, forgiveness, and generosity, which lie at the core of the Christmas story.

I have intentionally chosen Bible verses that illustrate a specific aspect of the Christmas story. Each verse serves as a foundation for the short meditation that follows, inspiring and deepening your understanding of the significance of Jesus' birth. You'll also gain a deeper understanding of the historical context and events surrounding the birth of Jesus and discover how His birth continues to impact your life today.

As you engage with the Scriptures and reflect on their significance, you will be equipped to share the joy and hope found in Jesus' birth with those around you. Your Christmas celebration will take on new meaning as you purposefully seek to extend love, grace, and compassion to your loved ones and even those who are difficult to love, mirroring the heart of God.

Allow the heart of God to touch your heart and experience the true spirit of Christmas. I pray these daily reflections guide your thoughts, prayers, and actions toward the profound and life-changing message of Jesus' birth.

I pray this Christmas season, you will be filled with more joy, hope, and peace than ever before. May the celebration of Jesus' birth permeate every aspect of your life, transforming your relationships with others. May you be inspired to share the love and message of Jesus, spreading the true spirit of Christmas far and wide.

And finally, may these daily Bible devotions help you focus on the true meaning of Christmas and draw you closer to the heart of God.

PLAYLIST

O Holy Night ~ David Phelps

Mary, Did You Know ~ Mark Lowry

Bethlehem Morning ~ Sandi Patty

Away In A Manager ~ Tommee Profitt, Daniel Saint Black, Ruelle

Little Drummer Boy ~ for KING & COUNTRY

We Three Kings ~ Celtic Woman

Light of the World ~ Lauren Daigle

Hark! The Herald Angels Sing ~ Jeremy Camp

Come, Thou Long-Expected Jesus ~ Voice Male

Joy to the World ~ Elevate Church Music, Alexis Tuiz

Isaiah 9 – Wonderful Counselor ~ Project of Love

Jesus, Light Of The World ~ Third Day

Romans 15:13 (Benediction Song) ~ Cheri Keaggy

Handel's Messiah ~ Choir of King's College

Love of God ~ MercyMe

Emmanuel God With Us – Live ~ Chris Tomlin

Joy ~ for KING & COUNTRY

Gift of Grace ~ Jessica King

He Is Here ~ ITOWN Worship

I Will Sing of Your Salvation ~ Francesca LaRosa

Birthday of a King/Extravagant ~Building 429

Jesus ~ Chris Tomlin

Scan the QR code below with your camera or follow the link for the playlist of all the songs found in this devotional. Let the music enrich your daily devotion.

The Prepare Him Room Playlist:

https://t.ly/PrepareHimRoomPlaylist

DAY 1

THE PROMISE OF A SAVIOR

Therefore the Lord himself will give you a sign: The virgin will conceive and give birth to a son, and will call him Immanuel.

Isaiah 7:14

During the Christmas season, we celebrate the fulfillment of a promise made centuries before the birth of Jesus Christ. In the book of Isaiah, a prophetic message foretells the coming of a Savior, a Messiah who would bring hope and redemption to the world.

We are reminded of God's incredible love and faithfulness. He promised to send His Son, born of a virgin, to be with us. This promise was fulfilled in the birth of Jesus, whose name, Immanuel, means "God with us."

I remember one Christmas when my family was going through a challenging time. We were facing financial struggles and dealing with a loss in our family. It seemed like there was little hope for joy and celebration during that season.

But as we gathered on Christmas Eve, we read the story of Jesus' birth and meditated on the promise of Immanuel. In our challenges, we found comfort in knowing God was with us. We experienced a sense of peace and hope that surpassed our circumstances.

That Christmas became a turning point for us as we embraced the promise of a Savior who brings light into darkness and restores hope amid despair. It reminded us that God is present no matter what we face, and His love never fails.

As we celebrate Christmas this year, let us hold onto the promise of a Savior. Let us remember that Jesus came to bring us salvation and eternal life. May His presence fill our hearts with joy, peace, and renewed hope.

PONDER

How does the promise of a Savior bring comfort and hope to your life? How can you share the promise of Jesus with others during this Christmas season?

PRAY

Heavenly Father, thank You for the promise of a Savior. Help me focus on the true meaning of Christmas and find peace and joy in the birth of Jesus. Amen.

DAY 2

THE DIVINE ANNOUNCEMENT

You will conceive and give birth to a son, and you are to call him Jesus. He will be great and will be called the Son of the Most High. The Lord God will give him the throne of his father David, and he will reign over Jacob's descendants forever; his kingdom will never end.

Luke 1:31–33

One Christmas, I felt lost and uncertain about the future. I was grappling with challenges, seeking guidance, and longing for a sense of purpose. As I read about the angel Gabriel appearing to Mary, I was struck by her faith and obedience. Despite the uncertainty and fear she must have felt, Mary embraced her calling with trust and surrender. She willingly accepted the divine plan, becoming an instrument for God's incredible work in the world.

At that moment, I realized that just as Mary found purpose and hope through her encounter with God, I could also experience the transformative power of faith. Additionally, I understood that God has a unique purpose for each of us. This means we actively fulfill that purpose, bringing meaning and significance to our lives. It reminds us to embrace our uniqueness and not compare ourselves to others.

Christmas is a time to remember that God's plans are greater than ours. It reminds us that God can bring light and hope even in our darkest moments. Just as the birth of Jesus brought joy and salvation to the world, it also serves as a reminder that God can bring new beginnings and redemption into our lives.

May we have the faith and courage to say "yes" to God's plans, even when they seem daunting. Like Mary, let us trust in God's promises and allow His love to guide us in every aspect of our lives.

May this Christmas be a time of renewal and transformation as we open our hearts to the wonder of the Annunciation and the gift of Jesus Christ.

PONDER

How does the story of the announcement of Jesus's birth inspire you to surrender to God's plan for your life? How can you demonstrate faith and courage, even when faced with uncertainty?

PRAY

Dear God, thank You for choosing Mary to be the mother of Jesus. Help me to have faith and obedience as Mary did and to trust Your plans for my life. Amen.

DAY 3

THE JOURNEY TO BETHLEHEM

*So Joseph also went up from the town of Nazareth in
Galilee to Judea, to Bethlehem the town of David, because he belonged to the house and line of David. He
went there to register with Mary, who was pledged to be
married to him and was expecting a child.*

Luke 2:4–5

It was a cold Christmas Eve, and I sat alone in my room, feeling
a sense of emptiness in my heart. The holiday cheer around me
only seemed to magnify my loneliness. As I gazed out the window, my
thoughts wandered to the story of Bethlehem and the birth of Jesus.
I realized that just like Bethlehem, my heart needed the presence of a
King. I needed Jesus in my life to fill the void within me.

During the time of Jesus, Bethlehem may not have been much of
a village. Still, it held significant importance as it was King David's
village. This connection to King David is essential because it helps
establish Jesus' heritage and lineage. Jesus is not just any successor

of David; he is THE successor. He is the one who reigns on David's throne forever, fulfilling the prophecies about the coming Messiah.

Even before Jesus arrived on the scene, His identity and role had already been revealed to us. He was destined to be the King! This was not a mere coincidence or an ordinary role but a divine appointment. Jesus came to establish a kingdom that would surpass any earthly kingdom. He came to reign with love, grace, and mercy, bringing salvation and eternal life to all who believe in Him.

As we celebrate the birth of Jesus, let us reflect on the significance of Bethlehem, the village where the King of kings was born. Let us invite Jesus, the King of Bethlehem, to reign in our hearts and transform our lives. May His love and grace fill us and guide us in every aspect of our journey. This Christmas, I encourage you to open your heart to Jesus and allow Him to bring His light and love into your life. He is the true King who can bring meaning and fulfillment to our lives, no matter what circumstances we may be facing.

PONDER

Do you submit your heart, desires, and will to Him? Do you recognize His authority and sovereignty?

PRAY

Dear God, thank you for the journey that led to the birth of Jesus. Help us to trust in Your faithfulness and purpose, even when we face challenges and uncertainties. Guide us on the paths that lead us closer to You and help us embrace our journeys. In Jesus' name, Amen.

DAY 4

NO ROOM IN THE INN

And she gave birth to her firstborn, a son. She wrapped
him in cloths and placed him in a manger, because there
was no guest room available for them.

Luke 2:7

One Christmas, we didn't have much to spare, so I explained to the children that they had to be creative with the gifts they would give each other. Instead of exchanging store-bought gifts, the children created gifts out of paper. One created a beauty set, which included a hairdryer and nail polish bottle. It was a humbling experience that reminded me of the true spirit of Christmas – giving, compassion, and connection.

Christmas is a time to reflect on the humble birth of Jesus Christ, the Son of God. The birth of Jesus was not a grand spectacle in a palace but a quiet and humble arrival in a stable. This reminds us that God's love knows no bounds and that He will meet us in the most ordinary and unexpected places.

The choice of a manger as Jesus' first bed is also significant. A manger is a feeding trough for animals, a symbol of sustenance and provision. It reminds us that Jesus came to nourish our souls and provide for our deepest needs. He is the bread of life, offering us spiritual sustenance that can satisfy our hunger and thirst like nothing else.

In our busy lives and extravagant celebrations, let us remember the true meaning of Christmas. It is a time to recognize and cherish the gift of Jesus, who came to bring hope, peace, and salvation to the world.

As we gather with loved ones and exchange gifts, may we also take a moment to reflect on the greatest gift of all – the gift of God's love through His Son, Jesus Christ. Let us embrace the spirit of humility, love, and gratitude this Christmas season, just as Jesus humbly entered the world.

PONDER

How can we embrace the unexpected ways God works in our lives? How can we demonstrate God's love for others during this Christmas season?

PRAY

Gracious God, thank You for reminding us of the inn's lack of room. Help us examine our hearts and make space for Jesus. Let us prioritize His presence above worldly distractions. Fill us with Your love, grace, and peace as we welcome Jesus into every aspect of our lives. In His name, Amen.

DAY 5

THE SHEPHERDS AND THE ANGELS

And the angel said to them, 'Fear not, for behold, I bring
you good news of great joy that will be for all the people.
For unto you is born this day in the city of David a
Savior, who is Christ the Lord.'

Luke 2:10–11 (ESV)

On that holy night, the angel brought an incredible message to the shepherds. The angel's words filled their hearts with hope and joy, for the angel announced the birth of a Savior—Jesus Christ, the Messiah.

In the hustle and bustle of the holiday season, it is easy to get caught up in the materialistic aspects of Christmas. But let us remember the true reason for our celebration—the birth of our Savior.

Jesus came into the world as a humble baby, born in a stable, yet his arrival brought great joy to everyone. He came to bring salvation, to reconcile us with God, and to offer us eternal life.

As we gather with family and friends, exchange gifts, and enjoy festive traditions, let us not forget the significance of this season. Let us take a moment to reflect on the love and grace that God has shown us through the gift of His Son.

May the joy and peace of Christmas fill your heart and home. May you experience the true meaning of this season as you celebrate the birth of our Savior, Jesus Christ.

PONDER

How has the birth of Jesus brought joy and hope into your life? In what ways can you prioritize the true meaning of Christmas?

PRAY

Heavenly Father, like the shepherds, may I be filled with joy and awe at the news of Jesus' birth. Help me to share this good news with others and to be a witness of Your love and grace. Amen.

DAY 6

THE VISIT OF THE WISE MEN

When they saw the star, they were overjoyed. On coming to the house, they saw the child with his mother Mary, and they bowed down and worshiped him. Then they opened their treasures and presented him with gifts of gold, frankincense, and myrrh.

Matthew 2:10–11

The Wise Men's visit to the baby Jesus holds deep spiritual meaning. These wise and learned individuals, guided by a miraculous star, traveled from afar to seek and worship the newborn King.

Their response upon finding Jesus was one of overwhelming joy. In the presence of the Savior, they humbly bowed down and offered their precious gifts as an act of worship. Their actions reflect their recognition of Jesus' divinity and their reverence and adoration for Him.

The gifts they presented hold symbolic significance. Gold represents Jesus' kingship and royalty, foreshadowing His future reign as the King of kings. Frankincense symbolizes His priesthood, signifying His role as the mediator between God and humanity. Myrrh, often used in burials, points to Jesus' sacrificial death and the redemption He would bring to the world.

Like the Wise Men, we should approach Him with joy, humility, and a desire to worship Him fully. Just as they brought their treasures, we can offer Him our hearts, talents, and lives, recognizing His sovereignty and surrendering to His will.

May we bow before Him with reverence and gratitude, acknowledging Him as our King, Priest, and Savior.

PONDER

Are you offering the best of yourself?

PRAY

Heavenly Father, we thank You for the Wise Men's visit and the profound message it carries. Help us to seek Jesus wholeheartedly, offering Him our worship and surrendering our lives to Him. May we always recognize Him as our King, Priest, and Savior. In Jesus' name, Amen.

DAY 7

THE LIGHT OF THE WORLD

In him was life, and that life was the light of all mankind. The light shines in the darkness, and the darkness has not overcome it.

John 1:4–5

The Gospel of John describes Jesus as the Light of the World. These verses remind us of the profound significance of this metaphor. Not only does Jesus bring life, but He also brings light to a dark and broken world.

Just as light dispels darkness, Jesus brings hope, peace, and understanding to our lives. In a world filled with chaos, confusion, and despair, His light shines brightly, guiding us on the path of righteousness.

The darkness may try to overpower the light, but it will never succeed. The light of Jesus is eternal and unyielding. It illuminates the darkest corners of our hearts, exposing sin and leading us to repentance and forgiveness.

As followers of Christ, we are called to reflect His light on those around us. We are to be beacons of hope, love, and truth in a world that desperately needs it. Through our words, actions, and attitudes, we can bring the light of Jesus into the lives of others.

We are not called to hide our light but to let it shine brightly. May we continuously draw closer to Jesus, allowing His light to transform us from within, and may His light radiate through us, bringing hope and pointing others to the true Light of the World.

PONDER

How can you personally embrace the light of Christ in your life? How can you share Christ's light with others during this Christmas season and beyond?

PRAY

Dear Heavenly Father, thank you for sending Jesus as the Light of the World. His light shines in the darkness. Fill us with hope, peace, and understanding, and guide us on His righteousness. Illuminate the darkest corners of our hearts, leading us to repentance and forgiveness. Help us to be vessels of Your light, reflecting Your light shine through us, bringing hope, and pointing others to the real Light, Jesus Christ. In His name, we pray. Amen.

DAY 8

THE WORD BECAME FLESH

*And the Word became flesh and dwelt among us, and
we have seen his glory, glory as of the only Son from the
Father, full of grace and truth.*

John 1:14

This verse illustrates the deep truth that God, in the person of
Jesus, took on human form and lived among us. This divine act
of love and humility is the cornerstone of our faith.

When we reflect on the Word becoming flesh, we are confronted with
the astounding reality of God's presence in our midst. The Almighty,
who created the heavens and the earth, chose to step into our broken
world, to experience our joys and sorrows, and to ultimately offer us
salvation.

We see the perfect blend of grace and truth in Jesus. His life was
marked by compassion, forgiveness, and selflessness. He demonstrated
the Father's boundless love, extending grace to the undeserving and
offering hope to the hopeless. At the same time, Jesus spoke truth with

authority, challenging societal norms and revealing the path to eternal life.

We can honor Jesus' birth by being kind and generous and sharing His love with others during this Christmas season. Whether volunteering, donating, or spending time with loved ones, these actions celebrate the impact of the Word-made flesh.

May we be reminded of God's love for us. Let us respond with gratitude and surrender, opening our hearts to the Word-made flesh and allowing His glory to shine through us. May we strive to live in His grace and truth, reflecting His character to the world around us.

PONDER

How can you show kindness and generosity during the Christmas season? What are some specific ways you can share the love and joy of Jesus with others during this special time of year?

PRAY

Heavenly Father, we thank You for the gift of Your Son, Jesus Christ, who became flesh and dwelt among us. We are in awe of Your love and humility shown through this act. Open our hearts to receive Your grace and truth. Help us surrender to You and follow Jesus. Fill us with Your presence and guide us. May Your glory shine through us as we live out the miracle of the incarnation. In Jesus' name, Amen.

DAY 9

THE HUMILITY OF JESUS

But emptied himself, by taking the form of a servant, being born in the likeness of men. And being found in human form, he humbled himself by becoming obedient to the point of death, even death on a cross.

Philippians 2:7–8 (ESV)

We are reminded of Jesus Christ's incredible humility during this Christmas season. Despite being the Son of God, He willingly emptied Himself and took on the role of a servant. Just as He humbly entered the world as a baby in a manger, He calls us to embrace the spirit of humility and selflessness.

As we celebrate the birth of our Savior, let us reflect on the true meaning of Christmas. It is not about extravagant gifts or elaborate feasts but about the humble arrival of Jesus into our lives. We are called to follow His example just as He came to serve and not to be served.

How can we display the humility of Jesus during this Christmas season?

- **Serve others**: Look for opportunities to help those in need, whether volunteering at a local shelter, reaching out to a lonely neighbor, or donating to a charitable cause. By selflessly serving others, we reflect the love of Christ.

- **Practice gratitude**: Take time to appreciate the blessings in your life and express gratitude to God and those around you. Recognize that every good gift comes from above and cultivate a heart of thankfulness.

Remember that Christmas's true joy lies in embracing Jesus's humility. As we seek to display His love and selflessness, may our actions reflect the true spirit of the Christmas season.

PONDER

How will you display the humility of Jesus during this Christmas season? How can you serve others and practice gratitude?

PRAY

Dear Lord, help us have humble hearts and servant's attitudes, following in Jesus' footsteps. Teach us to put others before ourselves, love sacrificially, and obey Your will. May Your Holy Spirit guide us to live a life of humility, just as Jesus did. In His name, we pray, Amen.

DAY 10

THE GIFT OF LOVE

This is how God showed his love among us: He sent his one and only Son into the world that we might live through him. This is love: not that we loved God, but that he loved us and sent his Son as an atoning sacrifice for our sins.

1 John 4:9–10

What an incredible gift of love that God has given us. God's love was shown by sending His Son, Jesus Christ, into the world. It is through Jesus that we find true life and salvation.

God's love is so amazing that it is not conditional on our love for Him. In fact, it was quite the opposite. He loved us even when we were undeserving and sent Jesus to be the ultimate sacrifice for our sins.

When we think about the depth and magnitude of God's love, it can be overwhelming. We may question why He loves us so much, especially when we fall short and make mistakes. That's the beauty of God's love;

it's not based on our performance or worthiness. God loves us simply because He is love, and He wants a relationship with us.

God's love is constant, unwavering, and everlasting. This knowledge should fill us with gratitude and awe, knowing that we are deeply loved by the Creator of the universe.

Just as God loved us, we are called to love others with that same self-lessness and compassion. Each day presents opportunities to extend God's love to those around us.

In a world that often values self-centeredness and personal gain, demonstrating God's love can be a powerful testimony to the trans-formative power of His grace. Through our actions, others can catch a glimpse of His love and experience His goodness. Let us intentionally seek ways to demonstrate God's love, knowing that our efforts can make a difference in someone's life, no matter how small.

PONDER

How can you show love to others this Christmas? How can you bring joy to those around you during this season of giving?

PRAY

Dear God, thank You for the incredible gift of Your love demonstrated through Jesus' birth and sacrifice. Help me to love others as You have loved me and to share Your love with those around me. Amen.

DAY 11

THE JOY OF SALVATION

But the angel said to them, 'Do not be afraid. I bring you
good news that will cause great joy for all the people.'
Luke 2:10

The angel proclaims the good news of Jesus' birth and brings not just ordinary joy but an overwhelming and immense joy that extends beyond measure to everyone on earth. The birth of Jesus, the Son of God, is not just a mere event but an extraordinary and awe-inspiring demonstration of God's infinite love and His divine plan for the redemption and salvation of mankind.

The joy of salvation is not restricted or confined to a privileged few. It is an all-encompassing and inclusive joy accessible to everyone who places their faith and trust in Jesus Christ. It is a joy that transcends the limitations of our circumstances, surpassing any hardship or tribulation we may face. It has the power to transform our hearts and fill us with unshakable hope and an enduring peace that surpasses all understanding.

Let us remind ourselves of the great and incomparable gift of salvation that God has graciously bestowed upon us through the sacrifice of His one and only Son. Let us wholeheartedly embrace and bask in the immeasurable joy that originates from the knowledge and assurance that we are unconditionally loved, completely forgiven, and eternally redeemed by our Heavenly Father.

Our joy should overflow from within and radiate to those around us, serving as a powerful testimony of the transformative power of a personal relationship with Jesus Christ. Let us not keep this life-changing good news to ourselves, but with enthusiasm and passion, seize every opportunity to share this glorious message of salvation with others so that they, too, may encounter and experience the overwhelming and boundless joy and love that comes from knowing and walking with Jesus Christ.

PONDER

Contemplate the incredible gift of salvation and the immeasurable love of God. How can you express gratitude for this gift and share it with others in meaningful ways during this Christmas season?

PRAY

Heavenly Father, thank You for the joy Jesus' birth brings our lives. May we experience the fullness of Your joy and share it with others so that they may come to know and experience the salvation found in Jesus. Amen.

DAY 12

Six Gifts from God

For to us a child is born, to us a son is given, and the government will be on his shoulders. And he will be called Wonderful Counselor, Mighty God, Everlasting Father, Prince of Peace.

Isaiah 9:6 (ESV)

Wonderful Counselor: The embodiment of wisdom and understanding Jesus is our guide and counselor. He offers us divine counsel and guidance in every aspect of our lives. He knows the deepest desires of our hearts and provides the perfect guidance to navigate life's challenges.

Mighty God: Jesus is not just a mere human being BUT the Almighty God in human form. He possesses unlimited power and authority. In Him, we find strength and protection. He is our refuge and fortress, mighty to save.

Everlasting Father: Jesus, the Son of God, reveals the heart of the Father to us. He perfectly represents God's love, compassion, and care.

As our Everlasting Father, He offers us eternal security, comfort, and provision. He cherishes and nurtures us as a loving father would.

Prince of Peace: Jesus brings us true and lasting peace in a troubled world. He reconciles us to God, restores our brokenness, and offers peace that surpasses understanding. We can find peace with God, others, and ourselves through Him.

Child Born: The birth of Jesus is a miraculous event that brought hope and salvation to humanity. He came as a humble child, born in a stable, to redeem and reconcile us to God. His birth represents the beginning of a new era where God's love and grace are available to all.

Son Given: God gave His only Son, Jesus, as a sacrificial gift for the forgiveness of our sins. We can receive forgiveness, redemption, and eternal life through His sacrifice. God's love for us is demonstrated in the gift of His Son, who willingly laid down His life for our salvation.

PONDER

How does the role of Jesus as the Prince of Peace bring comfort and hope to your life?

PRAY

Dear Lord, I thank You for the six gifts You gave us through Jesus, the Prince of Peace. May these gifts transform us to be instruments of Your love and peace in the world. In Jesus' name, we pray. Amen.

DAY 13

THE LIGHT IN THE DARKNESS

When Jesus spoke again to the people, he said, 'I am the light of the world. Whoever follows me will never walk in darkness, but will have the light of life.'

John 8:12 (EHV)

As we celebrate the birth of Jesus, we are reminded of the significance of His coming. In a world filled with darkness and uncertainty, Jesus came as the Light that brings hope, joy, and salvation.

Just as a single candle can illuminate a dark room, Jesus, the Light of the world, brings illumination to our lives. He guides us through the shadows of life, showing us the way to eternal life and a relationship with God.

As we gather with loved ones, exchange gifts, and partake in festive traditions, let us remember the true reason for the season. Let us remember that Jesus is the ultimate gift, the Light that pierces through the darkness of sin and despair.

May we open our hearts to receive the Light of Christ during this Christmas season. Let His love and grace shine brightly in our lives, illuminating every corner with hope, peace, and purpose. May we also share this Light with others, being beacons of love and kindness amidst a world that desperately needs it.

As we celebrate Christmas, let us embrace the truth that Jesus is the Light in the darkness. May His presence fill our hearts and homes with joy, and may His Light transform our lives forever.

PONDER

As you celebrate Christmas, how can you be a beacon of love and kindness, sharing the Light of Christ with others who may need hope and encouragement? Who in your circle needs to feel Christ's love and mercy?

PRAY

Heavenly Father, thank You for the Light of Jesus that shines in the darkness of this world. Guide my steps and lead me in righteousness as I follow Him. Amen.

DAY 14

THE GIFT OF HOPE

May the God of hope fill you with all joy and peace
as you trust in him, so that you may overflow with
hope by the power of the Holy Spirit.

Romans 15:13 (NIV)

God sent His Son to bring light and salvation during darkness and despair. The birth of Jesus fulfilled the prophecies and promises of the Old Testament, giving us hope for a better future. Jesus Christ is the ultimate gift of hope to the world.

In Romans 15:13, the apostle Paul reminds us that our hope comes from God. As believers, we have access to a never-ending source of hope through our trust in Him. This hope brings us joy and peace, even during challenging circumstances.

Christmas is when we reflect on the incredible love of God, who sent His Son to reconcile us to Himself. It is a time to remember that no matter what we face in life, we can find hope in Jesus. His birth reminds us that God is with us, guiding and protecting us every step of the way.

Hold onto the gift of hope that Jesus brings. Let us trust in Him and allow His Holy Spirit to fill us with overflowing hope, joy, and peace. May this hope shine brightly in our lives and be a source of encouragement to those around us.

The true meaning of Christmas is not found in material gifts or temporary pleasures. It is found in the gift of hope that God has given us through His Son, Jesus Christ. Embrace this gift, share it with others, and let the hope of Christmas transform your life.

PONDER

How does trusting in God bring joy and peace in your life? In what ways can you allow the Holy Spirit to fill you with hope?

PRAY

Dear God, thank You for the gift of hope in Jesus. May His hope fill my heart and overflow in my life, bringing joy and peace to those around me. Amen.

DAY 15

THE SAVIOR OF THE WORLD

*Today in the town of David a Savior has been born to
you; he is the Messiah, the Lord.*

Luke 2:11 (NIV)

In the Gospel of Luke, we are presented with the awe-inspiring
account of the birth of Jesus Christ, who is revered as the Savior of
the world. Luke 2:11 beautifully proclaims, "For unto you is born this
day in the city of David a Savior, who is Christ the Lord." This verse
not only unveils the majestic identity of Jesus as the Savior but also
illuminates the profound significance of His arrival into the world.

But who, truly, is this Savior? Jesus magnificently embodies God's
boundless love and immeasurable mercy. His purposeful coming was
to liberate humanity from the shackles of sin and to reconcile us with
God's divine presence. Through His extraordinary life, enlightening
teachings, and ultimately, His sacrificial offering upon the cross, Jesus
extends the gifts of redemption, forgiveness, and eternal life to all who
wholeheartedly embrace Him.

The question naturally arises: Why did He come? Jesus embarked upon His earthly journey to fulfill the divine plan of salvation. His divine mission was to bestow hope, peace, and reconciliation upon a deeply wounded world longing for restoration. The birth of Jesus marked the dawning of an extraordinary mission that sought to rescue humanity from the dire consequences of sin and offer the wonderful opportunity of a renewed, intimate relationship with the Almighty.

PONDER

How does knowing Jesus as the Savior bring hope and purpose to your life? How can you share the message of salvation with others during this Christmas season?

PRAY

Heavenly Father, thank You for sending Jesus as the world's Savior. Help me to surrender my life to Him and to share the good news of His salvation with others during this Christmas season. Amen.

DAY 16

THE LOVE OF GOD REVEALED

This is how God showed his love among us: He sent his one and only Son into the world that we might live through him.

1 John 4:9 (NIV)

God's love for us is revealed through the gift of His Son. Jesus came into the world to show us the depth of God's love and to offer us eternal life through Him. When we ponder on the magnitude of this act, we realize that God's love is not just a fleeting emotion or a distant concept but a tangible, sacrificial love that surpasses our understanding.

Through Jesus, God entered our human experience, sharing our joys and sorrows and empathizing with our struggles and pain. He walked among us, demonstrating compassion, forgiveness, and grace. Jesus showed us that God's love is not conditional or limited but unconditional and boundless.

Furthermore, Jesus' ultimate act of love was His sacrifice on the cross. He willingly laid down His life for us, taking on the weight of our sins and offering us redemption and reconciliation with God. This sacrificial love demonstrates God's desire for us to experience true life and relationship with Him.

As we focus on the love of God revealed through Jesus, we are reminded that His love is not limited to a specific season or time. It is a love that transcends all boundaries and is available daily. Let us strive to live in the light of this love, sharing it with others and allowing it to guide our thoughts, words, and actions. May the love of God continue to transform us and draw us closer to Him.

PONDER

There are always people in our lives who are difficult for us to love. Can we bury the hatchet or give up the judgment and love someone we have put off loving?

PRAY

Heavenly Father, we thank You for the love shown through Jesus Christ. Help us understand and experience Your love fully. Transform us, reminding us of our worth. Empower us to share Your love, especially during Christmas. Guide us to be kind, compassionate, and forgiving. Fill us with joy and hope, and strengthen our relationship with You. In Jesus' name, Amen.

DAY 17

THE GIFT OF FORGIVENESS

In him we have redemption through his blood, the forgiveness of sins, in accordance with the riches of God's grace.

Ephesians 1:7 (NIV)

As we celebrate the birth of Jesus, let us reflect on the incredible gift of forgiveness that God has given us through His Son. Ephesians 1:7 reminds us that in Jesus, we have redemption and the forgiveness of sins. Jesus paid the price for our sins through His sacrifice on the cross, offering us forgiveness and reconciliation with God.

The gift of forgiveness is a profound expression of God's love and grace towards us. It is not something we can earn or deserve, but it is freely given to us through Jesus' selfless act of love. Just as God has forgiven us, He calls us to extend forgiveness to others.

Christmas is a time of reconciliation and restoration. As we celebrate the birth of Jesus, let us remember that His coming into the world was the ultimate act of forgiveness. In the busyness and distractions of the holiday season, let's reflect on the forgiveness we have received and can offer others.

Let us forgive those who have wronged us, just as God has forgiven us. Let us release any bitterness, resentment, or grudges and choose to walk in the freedom that comes from being forgiven. As we extend forgiveness, we mirror the heart of God and allow His love to flow through us.

Let forgiveness be at the forefront of our hearts and minds this Christmas. May we experience the transformative power of God's forgiveness in our lives and be agents of forgiveness to those around us. As we embrace the gift of forgiveness, we can genuinely celebrate the true meaning of Christmas and the abundant grace that God has poured out upon us.

PONDER

Is there someone in your life whom you need to extend forgiveness to? How can you take steps towards forgiveness and reconciliation?

PRAY

extend that same forgiveness to others and Heavenly Father, thank You for the incredible gift of forgiveness through Jesus' sacrifice on the cross. Please help us walk in the freedom that comes from being forgiven. Fill our hearts with Your love and grace, and help us to reflect Your forgiveness to those around us. In Jesus' name, Amen.

DAY 18

THE GOOD NEWS OF GREAT JOY

But the angel said to them, 'Do not be afraid. I bring you
good news that will cause great joy for all the people.'
Luke 2:10 (NIV)

The angel's message was filled with hope and joy, offering a glimmer of light in a world longing for redemption. But what is this good news?

The good news the angel shared was the arrival of a Savior, Jesus Christ, who would bring salvation to all people. This news was not limited to a select few but was meant for everyone, regardless of their background, status, or past mistakes. It was an invitation to experience the love, forgiveness, and abundant life found in a relationship with Jesus.

The birth of Jesus marked a turning point in human history. It was the fulfillment of God's promise to send a Messiah, the One who would reconcile humanity with God and restore the broken relationship caused by sin. Through Jesus' life, death, and resurrection, we have the opportunity to be forgiven, redeemed, and restored to a right relationship with God.

The good news of Jesus' birth brings great joy because it offers hope, peace, and eternal life. It reminds us that we are not alone in our struggles and that God is with us every step of the way. It assures us that there is always a way back to God, no matter how far we may have wandered. It brings comfort and assurance that we are loved unconditionally and that our lives have purpose and meaning.

As we reflect on the good news of Jesus' birth, let us be filled with joy and gratitude. Let us share this good news with others so they may experience the transformative power of God's love and grace. Let us remember that the true meaning of Christmas is found in the birth of Jesus, the Savior who brings hope, joy, and everlasting life.

This Christmas season, spread the good news that Jesus came to save all people!

PONDER

How does the good news of Jesus' birth bring joy and hope to your life? How can you share Jesus' good news with others during this Christmas season?

PRAY

Heavenly Father, thank You for the good news of Jesus' birth, which brings great joy. Help us fully embrace this good news and share it with others. Fill our hearts with Your love and joy this Christmas season and always. In Jesus' name, Amen.

DAY 19

THE GIFT OF GRACE

For the grace of God has appeared that offers salvation to all people.

Titus 2:11 (NIV)

Grace is a gift freely given by God, unearned and undeserved. It is His divine favor and loving-kindness extended to humanity despite our shortcomings and failures. The birth of Jesus is the ultimate expression of God's grace, as He came to offer us salvation and reconciliation with God.

In a world that often operates on merit and works, it is a beautiful and humbling realization that we cannot earn or achieve God's grace. It is a gift that transcends our efforts and accomplishments. Instead, it is rooted in God's love and mercy, flowing from His generous heart.

The gift of God's grace is transformative. It has the power to forgive our sins, cleanse us from unrighteousness, and bring us into a new and restored relationship with our Heavenly Father. We are saved and made new through God's grace, finding true freedom and purpose in life.

As we celebrate Christmas, let us embrace the gift of God's grace with gratitude and humility. Let us recognize that it is not something we can earn or achieve but something freely given by God out of His great love for us. May we fully embrace the salvation offered through Jesus Christ and allow His grace to transform and renew our lives.

As recipients of God's grace, let us show grace to others. Just as we have received forgiveness and mercy, let us offer the same to those around us, reflecting the heart of our Savior.

May we fully experience and appreciate the gift of God's grace this Christmas. May it fill our hearts with joy, peace, and gratitude. And may we, in turn, extend that same grace to others, embodying the true spirit of Christmas.

PONDER

How does understanding and receiving God's grace impact your relationship with Him? In what ways can you extend grace to others this Christmas season?

PRAY

Heavenly Father, thank You for the incredible gift of Your grace through Jesus Christ. Help us to fully embrace and live in the freedom of Your grace, extending it to others. Fill our hearts with gratitude for Your unmerited favor, and empower us to reflect Your grace in our words and actions. In Jesus' name, Amen.

DAY 20

THE PROMISE FULFILLED

All this took place to fulfill what the Lord had said through the prophet: 'The virgin will conceive and give birth to a son, and they will call him Immanuel' (which means 'God with us').

Matthew 1:22–23 (NIV)

Matthew 1:22-23 captures the fulfillment of a long-awaited promise from God. Centuries before the birth of Jesus, the prophet Isaiah prophesied about a miraculous sign—a virgin conceiving and giving birth to a son, whom they would call Immanuel, meaning "God with us." This prophecy spoke of a divine intervention that would forever change the course of humanity.

The birth of Jesus fulfills this extraordinary promise. God orchestrated His Son's miraculous conception and birth through the virgin Mary in His infinite wisdom and love. Through this miraculous event, God revealed His plan to dwell among His people, to be with them tangibly and intimately.

The realization of this promise is a powerful testament to God's faithfulness. It reminds us that God keeps His word, even when it seems impossible or unlikely. It demonstrates His deep desire to be in a relationship with us, to bridge the gap between heaven and earth, and to offer us salvation and eternal life.

The name Immanuel holds deep significance. It represents God's divine presence among His people. It reminds us that God is not distant or detached but intimately involved in our lives. He walks with us through every season, every joy, and every challenge. He is present in our celebrations and comforts us in our sorrows. Immanuel assures us we are never alone, for God is with us.

Remember our Heavenly Father's incredible love and grace as we reflect on the promise fulfilled in Matthew 1:22-23. He sent His Son, Jesus, to be Immanuel, the embodiment of His presence and love. Through Jesus, we have access to a personal relationship with God, experiencing His forgiveness, guidance, and peace.

May the fulfillment of this promise bring comfort and assurance to our hearts. May it deepen our faith and trust in God's promises. And may we live each day with the awareness that Immanuel, God with us, is present in every aspect of our lives.

PONDER

How does knowing that God is with you impact your daily life? How can you become more aware of God's presence in your life during this Christmas season?

PRAYER

Dear Lord, thank You for fulfilling Your promise to send a Savior. Help me recognize Your presence in my life and live with the assurance that You are always with me. Amen.

DAY 21

THE GIFT OF SALVATION

For God so loved the world that he gave his one and only Son, that whoever believes in him shall not perish but have eternal life.

John 3:16 (NIV)

In this well-known verse, we are confronted with the truth that God's love knows no bounds. He loved the world so much that He willingly sent His one and only Son to be our Savior. Jesus came to offer us the gift of eternal life, a life transformed by His love, grace, and forgiveness.

The gift of salvation is not something that we can earn or achieve on our own merit. It is a gift freely given by God, motivated by His unconditional love for us. Through faith in Jesus Christ, we can receive this gift and experience the fullness of life that comes from being reconciled to God.

Christmas is a powerful reminder of the lengths God went to redeem us. He humbly entered the world as a vulnerable baby, born in a manger, to be the ultimate sacrifice for our sins. Jesus' birth marked the beginning of a grand plan of salvation, culminating in His death and resurrection.

As we reflect on the gift of salvation, let us remember the magnitude of God's love and the great sacrifice that Jesus made on our behalf. We can find forgiveness, hope, and eternal life through His sacrifice. Our response to this gift is to believe in Jesus, to trust in Him, and to surrender our lives to His lordship.

This Christmas, let us celebrate Jesus's birth and embrace the gift of salvation that He offers. As we receive this gift, may it transform our lives and overflow into the lives of others. Let us share the good news of Jesus' birth and the gift of salvation with those around us so that they, too, may experience the joy and hope found in a relationship with Him.

PONDER

How does the gift of salvation through Jesus Christ impact your life? How can you share the gift of salvation with others during this Christmas season?

PRAY

Heavenly Father, thank You for the gift of salvation through Jesus Christ. May we never take this incredible gift for granted and share it with others so that they, too, may have eternal life in You. Amen.

DAY 22

THE BIRTH OF A KING

Today in the town of David a Savior has been born to you; he is the Messiah, the Lord. This will be a sign to you: You will find a baby wrapped in cloths and lying in a manger.

Luke 2:11–12 (NIV)

The birth of Jesus, the King of kings, is a momentous event that forever changed the course of history. We are told of the miraculous birth of Jesus in the town of David. This humble birth was not just the arrival of an ordinary baby; it marked the coming of the long-awaited Messiah, the Lord and Savior of the world.

The birth of a king is often associated with grandeur, power, and wealth. However, Jesus, the King of kings, entered the world in the most humble and unexpected way. Wrapped in swaddling cloths and laid in a manger, He embraced a life of humility and selflessness from the beginning.

In Jesus, we see the perfect embodiment of love, grace, and truth. He came to bring salvation to all people, offering forgiveness and reconciliation with God. As the King of kings, He rules with right-eousness, justice, and compassion. His kingdom is not of this world but encompasses every heart that believes in Him.

The birth of Jesus is a reminder of God's incredible love for humanity. He sent His Son, the King of kings, to dwell among us, to experience the joys and sorrows of human life, and to ultimately offer Himself as a sacrifice for our sins. Through His birth, life, death, and resurrection, Jesus fulfilled the prophecies and promises of the Old Testament, bringing hope and salvation to all who believe in Him.

May we bow in adoration and surrender before the manger, acknowl-edging Jesus as our King and Lord. Let us embrace His teachings, follow His example, and obey His will. As we do so, we become citizens of His kingdom, experiencing the peace, joy, and abundant life He offers.

PONDER

How does understanding Jesus as the King of kings impact your view of His birth and life? How can you submit your life to the Lordship of Jesus, embracing His teachings and following His example?

PRAY

Dear God, thank You for the birth of Jesus, the King of kings. May I submit my life to His Lordship and follow Him wholeheartedly.

Amen.

DAY 23

THE GIFT OF PEACE

Peace I leave with you; my peace I give you. I do not
give to you as the world gives. Do not let your hearts be
troubled and do not be afraid.

John 14:27 (NIV)

The peace that Jesus gives is not temporary or fleeting; it is a deep and abiding peace that surpasses all understanding. It can calm our troubled hearts and bring rest to our weary souls. It remains steadfast despite life's storms and challenges.

The world may promise peace through material possessions, success, or temporary pleasures. But the peace that Jesus gives is different. It transcends circumstances and is rooted in a personal relationship with Him. It comes from knowing that we are loved, forgiven, and accepted by our Heavenly Father.

The gift of peace that Jesus offers is twofold. First, it is peace with God. Jesus made a way for us to be reconciled to God through His birth, life, death, and resurrection. He has taken the punishment for our sins and offered us forgiveness and eternal life instead. When we accept Him as our Savior, we experience true peace with God, knowing that we are in the right relationship with Him.

Second, it is the peace of God. As we abide in Christ and surrender our lives to Him, His peace fills our hearts and minds. It guards us against worry, anxiety, and fear. It sustains us in times of uncertainty and gives us hope for the future. It is a peace that surpasses all human understanding and can only come from God.

During the busyness and chaos of the Christmas season, pause and embrace the gift of peace that Jesus offers. Let's invite His peace to dwell within us, bringing calmness to our souls and harmony to our relationships. As we experience His peace, let us also be instruments of peace in our families, communities, and the world around us.

May the gift of peace that Jesus gives fill your heart this Christmas and New Year. May His peace guard your mind and guide your steps. May you reflect His peace, shining His light in a world needing His calming presence.

PONDER

How does the gift of peace that Jesus offers differ from the peace that the world promises? How can you experience and share the peace of Christ with someone this Christmas season?

PRAY

Heavenly Father, thank You for the gift of Your peace that surpasses all understanding. Help me to trust in You and to find rest and peace during life's challenges. Amen.

Die Geburt Jesu Christi in Bethlehem
Mt 1,18-25; Gal 4,4

2 Es begab sich aber in jenen Tagen, daß ein Befehl ausging von dem Kaiser Augustus“, daß der ganze Erdkreis sich erfassen‘ lassen sollte.

2 Diese Erfassung war die erste und geschah, als Kyrenius Statthalter in Syrien war.

3 Und es zogen alle aus, um sich erfassen zu lassen, jeder in seine eigene Stadt.

4 Es ging aber auch Joseph von Galiläa, aus der Stadt Nazareth, hinauf nach Judäa in die Stadt Davids, die Bethlehem heißt, weil er aus dem Haus und Geschlecht Davids war,

5 um sich erfassen zu lassen mit Maria, seiner ihm angetrauten Frau, die schwanger war.

6 Es geschah aber, während sie dort waren, da erfüllten sich die Tage, daß sie gebären sollte.

2 *Erfassung*
Apg 5,37

4 *Bethlehem*
1Sam 17,12;
Jub 7,42;
Davids
Mt 1,1.16;

LUKAS 2

14 Herrlichkeit [ist] bei Gott in der Höhe und Friede auf Erden, und unter den Menschen [Gottes] Wohlgefallen.

15 Und es geschah, als die Engel von ihnen weg in den Himmel zurückgekehrt waren, da sprachen die Hirten zueinander: Laßt uns doch bis nach Bethlehem gehen und die Sache sehen, die da geschehen ist, die der Herr uns verkündigt hat.

16 Und sie gingen eilends und fanden Maria und Joseph, dazu das Kind in der Krippe liegend.

17 Nachdem sie es aber gesehen hatten, machten sie das Wort bekannt, das ihnen über dieses Kind gesagt worden war.

DAY 24 & 25

THE BIRTH OF JESUS

While they were there, the time came for her to deliver
her child. And she gave birth to her firstborn son and
wrapped him in bands of cloth, and laid him in a
manger, because there was no place for them in the inn.
                                        Luke 2:6–7 (NIV)

L uke uses two sentences and a couple of dozen words to describe the birth of Jesus, the Son of God. It's not quite what we would expect for the birth of a king, THE KING OF KINGS. But I think that is the point.

Have you ever wondered what Mary and Joseph thought and felt as they traveled to Bethlehem? And how did they feel when they arrived and could not find a room at the inn? We don't know their plan after arriving in Bethlehem. Still, I'm sure it didn't include Mary giving birth in a stable and laying Jesus in a feeding trough for animals.

No matter what Jesus' crib was, His birth was no less miraculous, nor did it make His arrival on earth less meaningful. Even though things may not have gone as planned, it was still a powerful moment that ultimately changed life as we know it.

Tomorrow, as your friends and family gather and you are orchestrating a feast for everyone, ensuring they experience the holiday they are hoping for, I invite you to pause. During this pause, stop thinking about what comes next or what you couldn't get done. **PAUSE**. Set aside your plan. Breathe deep in the **HOPE** of a newborn Savior. Remember the **PEACE** that His birth has brought. Celebrate the **JOY** that came with His arrival. And most importantly, share the **LOVE** that inspired it all.

PONDER

How do the unexpected humble circumstances surrounding Jesus' birth emphasize the significance of His arrival as the Son of God? How can we find hope, peace, joy, and love in the story of Jesus' birth despite the challenges and uncertainties that may arise in our own lives?

PRAY

Heavenly Father, as we celebrate the birth of Jesus, may our hearts be filled with worship and adoration. Help us keep Jesus at the center of our Christmas celebrations and to share His love with others. Amen.

SCRIPTURE REFERENCES

Day 1 – Isaiah 7:14 (NIV)

Day 2 – Luke 1:31-33 (NIV)

Day 3 – Luke 2:4–5 (NIV)

Day 4 – Luke 2:7 (NIV)

Day 5 – Luke 2:10–11 (ESV)

Day 6 – Matthew 2:10–11 (NIV)

Day 7 – John 1:4–5 (NIV)

Day 8 – John 1:14 (NIV)

Day 9 – Philippians 2:7–8 (ESV)

Day 10 – 1 John 4:9–10 (NIV)

Day 11 – Luke 2:10 (NIV)

Day 12 – Isaiah 9:6 (ESV)

Day 13 – John 8:12 (EHV)

Day 14 – Romans 15:13 (NIV)

Day 15 – Luke 2:11 (NIV)

Day 16 – 1 John 4:9 (NIV)

Day 17 – Ephesians 1:7 (NIV)

Day 18 – Luke 2:10 (NIV)

Day 19 – Titus 2:11 (NIV)

Day 20 – Matthew 1:22–23 (NIV)

Day 21 – John 3:16 (NIV)

Day 22 – Luke 2:11–12 (NIV)

Day 23 – John 14:27 (NIV)

Day 24 & Day 25 – Luke 2:6–7 (NIV)

Visit Ruth's website for more information—podcast, blog, videos,
free resources, and the latest news.
www.ruthhovsepian.com

To book Ruth for your next event, Bible study, retreat, or conference,
visit www.ruthhovsepian.com or email info@ruthhovsepian.com.